"Sustainable, practical tools to help heal the suffering of any traumatic loss. Through mindful exploration of the landscape of grief—especially conditioned beliefs and feelings—the authors compassionately and wisely guide readers on an alchemical path of transformation and healing. Each chapter offers helpful exercises for processing the journey. Highly recommended for anyone looking to move beyond the paralysis of grief."

—**Beth Witrogen, MJ**, Pulitzer-nominated health care
    journalist, author of *Caregiving*, and contributing editor
    at *Journal on Active Aging*

"*How to Grieve What We've Lost* lives up to its title and will help any person who reads it. The exercises are presented clearly, and techniques for early grief provide grounding to help navigate difficult emotions. How to find meaning again and ways to handle difficult issues are addressed with gentle understanding. The compassionate therapists who collaborated to write this guide have created a book filled with gentle wisdom."

—**Claudia Coenen**, grief counselor; and author of *Shattered
    by Grief, Karuna Cards, The Creative Toolkit for Working
    with Grief and Bereavement*, and *Seasons of Grief*

"Discover your courage and compassion through *How to Grieve What We've Lost*, an essential guide for anyone experiencing loss. Rooted in a therapeutic approach, this book blends reflective and actionable exercises meeting you wherever you are on your unique grief journey. In the face of great change, this invaluable resource supports you in opening to the tenderness, resilience, and wisdom of your own heart."

—**Sharon Salzberg**, author of *Lovingkindness* and *Real Life*

T0000730

How to Grieve What We've Lost

EVIDENCE-BASED SKILLS *to* PROCESS GRIEF & RECONNECT WITH WHAT MATTERS

RUSS HARRIS • ALEXANDRA KENNEDY, LMFT

SAMEET M. KUMAR, PHD • MARY BETH WILLIAMS, PHD • SOILI POIJULA, PHD

New Harbinger Publications, Inc.

Publisher's Note

This publication is designed to provide accurate and authoritative information in regard to the subject matter covered. It is sold with the understanding that the publisher is not engaged in rendering psychological, financial, legal, or other professional services. If expert assistance or counseling is needed, the services of a competent professional should be sought.

NEW HARBINGER PUBLICATIONS is a registered trademark of New Harbinger Publications, Inc.

New Harbinger Publications is an employee-owned company.

Copyright © 2024 by Russ Harris, Alexandra Kennedy, Sameet M. Kumar, Mary Beth Williams, and Soili Poijula
New Harbinger Publications, Inc.
5720 Shattuck Avenue
Oakland, CA 94609
www.newharbinger.com

All Rights Reserved

Cover design by Sara Christian

Interior design by Michele Waters-Kermes

Acquired by Ryan Buresh

Edited by Amber Williams

FSC
www.fsc.org
MIX
Paper | Supporting
responsible forestry
FSC® C008955

Library of Congress Cataloging-in-Publication Data on file

Printed in the United States of America

26   25   24

10   9   8   7   6   5   4   3   2   1   First Printing

Contents

Introduction

The past few years have brought forth a tremendous amount of stress for all of us. In particular, our experiences with illness, conflict, and death have brought us intimately close to loss. Maybe it was a friend, a parent, family member, coworker, or someone else close to you. Regardless, I would be hard-pressed to find anyone who hasn't recently lost an important part of their life. Moreover, our society has undergone such rapid change in response to the COVID-19 pandemic that we have yet to properly mourn how many of us lost not just a person, but also the ways of life we considered "normal," our livelihoods, even our sense of who we are.

Grief, loss, and bereavement can be complicated experiences to manage and process. On the one hand, emotional pain, devastation, emptiness, and sadness are normal experiences that every person on the planet will go through; on the other, we can feel incredibly isolated, lonely, and confused. It can be hard to know the line between mourning the loss of someone or something in ways that are meaningful and being trapped in cycles of silence, avoidance, and poor mental health.

For that reason, we thought it helpful to assemble the most effective psychological tools for you to work with and process your loss in ways that should bring clarity and emotional peace. The exercises in this book have all been well researched and widely tested on hundreds, if not thousands, of people who sought help for their feelings of grief, mourning, and bereavement, and thus we feel that we can safely say that at least one thing in this book will work for you. The techniques herein come from respected therapeutic approaches that you may have heard of: cognitive behavior therapy, acceptance and commitment therapy, dialectical behavior therapy, grief counseling, and behavioral activation. It is our sincere hope that they provide structure for your grief journey.

Some of the exercises directly address particular kinds of loss; others are more holistic in nature. The practices at the beginning of the book are best for when your grief feelings are raw and fresh. But this book is not really meant to be read cover to cover. All the techniques in this book can be used in a moment's notice—as needed and on demand. So feel free to jump in and out. Perhaps leaving the book on the coffee table—or somewhere else where it is readily available—can help you find relief when you need it. Also, note there may be activities that won't suit you. You are not required to try everything. Nor are you expected to start reading this book immediately after experiencing your loss. The exercises in part 3 can be useful wherever you are on the journey. Finally, if you are dealing with intense feelings and mental distress, there are tools for common problems associated with loss in part 4; try those first.

The process of working through grief will ultimately present you with uncomfortable feelings. It is important to have an attitude of compassion as you process your feelings. Loss is a fundamental part of being alive and, if it's worked with in a gentle way, it can become a wellspring of meaning—ultimately clarifying for us how we wish the remainder of our lives to be. So, be careful and delicate with yourself.

PART 1

Strategies for Immediate Relief

Even the most expected loss comes swiftly and without warning. Our loss becomes like a storm that has blown our life off course, resulting in winds of intense emotion and troubling thoughts. This can be true in a moment's notice, even when the loss was experienced many years ago. Learning tools to meet these feelings and thoughts before they get out of hand is crucial—not only for day-to-day functioning but also for putting yourself in the right headspace to honor your grief and find meaning in your life.

GRIEF RESIDES IN YOUR HEART AND BELLY; IF YOU WANT TO HEAL, GENTLY LET YOUR ATTENTION DROP INTO YOUR BODY.

Create a Sanctuary

What to Know

The sanctuary is a powerful yet simple strategy for healing our grief without feeling overwhelmed. If we create a sacred space that gently holds us as we turn within, it sustains us as we move through the stages of grief. And it enables us to honor our grief for a limited time each day in the midst of our busy lives. Rather than feeling overwhelmed, those who use the sanctuary find that they have much more focus and energy for their work, schoolwork, friends, and families.

Why is the sanctuary so effective? What makes it so transformative?

- It creates a safe, insulated, contained space. This container holds and builds the energy necessary for transformation and healing in the psyche.

- It is time limited. Many people are willing to embrace uncomfortable states of being (such as grief) when there is a clear time limit.

- It allows us to go deep enough to heal.

- It is empowering to use—anyone, including children, can use it. Those who use it discover that once-frightening or troubling emotional states can be embraced more effectively in small bits.

- Using the sanctuary regularly generates a sense of peace in the midst of grieving. This provides the incentive to use it daily.

What to Do

Select a physical space in your home. It can be a nook, like a closet, or a piece of furniture, like a bench in your garden. The key is that the place must be solely devoted to being a sanctuary.

Be creative, thoughtful, and daring in creating your sanctuary. Let it be a place that inspires, comforts, and nurtures you in your grief. It's important that you will not be interrupted. Removed from the demands and distractions of your daily life, the sanctuary is a refuge dedicated to your healing and peace of mind.

If you find that you don't feel at ease in a location, move the sanctuary to another place. Most people need to try out different places until they settle on one that works. For example, you might not feel comfortable in a small, enclosed room; you might choose instead a sheltered corner of your garden as a sanctuary.

After finding the place for your sanctuary, create a specific area that you can focus on when you sit in the sanctuary. Think of this as a small personal altar that honors your grief. Arrange pictures, flowers, stones, shells, jewelry, candles, pieces of fabric, bowls, small statues, or whatever you feel connects you to your loss. Feel free to rearrange your altar regularly; you might find that what you want in your sanctuary changes as you move through your grief.

Once you have your sanctuary arranged, set a regular time for using it daily. Experiment with this until you find a time of the day that works best for you. The important thing is to use it daily so that there is a rhythm of turning within, then returning to your daily life.

If you feel anxious about using the sanctuary, start with ten minutes or less. Shorter, more focused times in the sanctuary may work better than longer periods, which might overwhelm you emotionally, at least at first. But ultimately, however long you practice, the key is to turn your attention within and deepen into whatever is taking place inside you during that session. It is the depth we access when we grieve that heals the psyche—not the length of time in the sanctuary.

As you enter the sanctuary each day, make sure that you won't be disturbed. Put a note on your door; turn off the phone. You are now entering a sacred space of grieving. Think of the sanctuary as a cocoon that holds and protects you while you are in a vulnerable state of transformation and change, much as the cocoon protects the caterpillar as it transforms into a butterfly.

Sit down. Take a couple of deep breaths, soften your belly, and settle into your sanctuary. Take a few minutes to let your eyes pass over pictures and objects you have placed on your altar. As your eyes linger there, let the reality sink in that your loss has indeed occurred; it takes time to fully absorb this.

If you are dealing with multiple losses, the fear of being overwhelmed is magnified. Dedicate each session in the sanctuary to one loss. Put out pictures and objects related to the loss you are focusing on that day. Stay with each loss for as long as it takes to feel some inner shift or healing. Then turn to the next loss.

Checking In
with Your Breath

What to Know

It is important that you learn how to notice how you feel in your body and mind and how you react when you remember, work on, or deal with the experiences of loss that have happened to you. It may take practice for you to focus on your body and your emotions and become aware of how you are reacting. And that is okay. This is a process. Imperfections are allowed.

What to Do

The following steps will help you check in with yourself and your breath:

1. Stop whatever activity you might be doing.

2. Sit quietly for a short period of time.

3. Turn your attention inward and ask your body how it feels.

4. Notice if you feel any tension anywhere in your body (for instance, in your shoulders, stomach, jaw, or back).

5. Notice if you are holding your breath.

6. Notice if you are doing any behaviors that suggest tension (biting your nails or picking at your skin).

7. Now notice any emotions you feel, if you are able to recognize them (fearful, sad, angry, lonely, and more).

8. Notice if you have racing thoughts or if you are able to stay focused.

If you've noticed any of the reactions listed above, take some time to practice the following deep breathing exercise.

1. Lie down on a blanket or rug on the floor. Bend your knees up toward you and move your feet until they are about eight inches apart, with your toes turned slightly outward. Keep your spine as straight as possible.

2. Scan your entire body and identify any places that hold tension.

3. Put one hand on your abdomen and one on your chest.

4. Inhale slowly through your nose into your abdomen so that it pushes your hand up; your chest should move only a little bit. Hold your breath while you count to five.

5. Smile slightly and then exhale through your mouth, taking as long as possible. Make a shushing sound as you exhale.

6. Repeat this at least five times, perhaps eventually increasing the amount of time you spend deep breathing to five to ten minutes.

7. When you've finished the exercise, again scan your entire body to see if any tension remains.

Once you are familiar with the technique, you can also use it while you are sitting or standing, whenever you feel tension in your body.

Staying Grounded

What to Know

The word "grounded" means staying present in the current moment, in contrast to "spacing out" or dissociating when things come up that remind you of your loss or of painful past experiences.

There are many suggestions as to how to remain grounded. Some of these include:

- breathing to bring yourself back to your body in the present moment

- using all your senses to be aware of your physical environment, and then talking to others about it

- being aware of your physical body and how you look

- being aware of your movements in space as you walk

- exercising while being aware of what you are doing

- making a plan for the day and sharing that plan with another

- challenging yourself to a contest to increase the length of time you can remain in the present

- watching television and telling yourself or others what you saw

- doing routine activities in a different way; for example, cleaning up the house in a different order than you usually do

- asking others to help you stay connected to them

- talking to yourself about the present

- planting your feet as firmly as you can on the ground in the here and now

What to Do

What cues do you have as to whether you are physically, emotionally, mentally, or spiritually grounded? Or what cues do you have to indicate that you're *not* grounded—that you're lost in feelings of grief or stress? Reflecting on the following questions in a journal will help you look at what you need.

- What makes you feel grounded physically when you are alone? With others? In different situations?

- When do you feel the most grounded?

- At which moments do you struggle with dissociation? With feeling spaced out, lost, hopeless, or helpless? How might grounding help you in those moments?

- Are those with whom you live or interact grounded? If they are, what makes those people safe? If they are not, are there ways you could change those relationships or better take care of yourself within them, to protect your sense of safety and presence?

- What can you do about your home to make it more grounded—a space that helps you stay in the present moment and feel safe, rather than under threat?

More to Do

The next time you're in one of the situations you wrote about, and struggling to stay present, try a grounding strategy.

If you struggle with the practice, or you find it doesn't work as well as you might've hoped, it's okay. Just stick with it. Grief can be a very powerful force. It can take time to reconnect with your body and the present moment when you've been struggling with it.

Handling Grief Triggers with Radical Acceptance

What to Know

Going through the first year of holidays and milestones without a loved one, or after your circumstances have irreparably changed, can be one of the most difficult tasks of your life after loss. Rather than avoiding triggers of acute grief—the situations, thoughts, emotions, urges, sensations, and memories that bring your feelings of grief to the surface—strive to understand the role that these triggers play, and what roles acute and subtle grief play in your life. As distressing as these triggers can be, it is through them that the task of grieving is accomplished. These triggers mark the turns in the spiral staircase of your grief.

During the first year or so after a loss, you may feel completely alone and vulnerable in the world. You may feel as if you are starting the grief process all over again around each special occasion or milestone. Whenever we are confronted with intense pain and distress, our first reaction is usually to try to run away from it. We continue to try to seek pleasure and avoid pain, even when we are told that our pain is normal; it sure doesn't feel okay, even if it is normal.

But what we do with our pain at this emotionally intense time is very important. If we choose to hide from our pain, we only lie to ourselves. And the pain comes out somehow, no matter how hard we try to suppress it. If it is blocked off or numbed, we'll be blind to the reason we're feeling the way we feel.

What to Do

So what do you do with the pain of grief? You certainly can't run from it, at least not permanently. Nor can you dwell in your pain indefinitely. What you *can* do, counterintuitive—and frightening—as it may seem, is turn around and embrace the process. This act of embracing is called *radical acceptance.*

This form of acceptance is called "radical" because it is completely unconditional. Nothing is turned away; all is welcome. Through radical acceptance, we learn that feelings we struggle with will never just "go away," they must be accepted—and when we *do* accept them, and allow them to be as they are, there's potential to heal from them.

To practice radical acceptance, you can say this mantra to yourself:

I am reminded by _____ (your trigger) that I have experienced a tremendous loss. I feel _____ (your feeling). These feelings are intense in the moment, but like all things they will fade. I welcome these feelings because they remind me that I loved _____ (what you lost) deeply.

You can still experience stress and distress, as well as happiness and pleasure; the world will keep going on. But your attitude toward it, and the way you approach your distress, will change. Even though we may not be able to avoid triggers of acute grief, the radical acceptance we can learn through the practice of mindfulness—the nonjudgmental awareness of all that's arising for us in the present moment—can dispel some of the suffering that grief can cause, particularly when we fight against what we feel. By changing your attitude toward suffering from one of confrontation to one of acceptance, you may in fact diminish your suffering.

Anchor Activities

What to Know

Are you struggling with triggers, dreams, nightmares, or intrusive thoughts in the wake of a loss or a stressful time of life? One way to gain some control over these internal phenomena is to use an *anchor*. Rothschild describes an anchor as "a concrete, observable resource," or one that is outside your own mind (2000, 91). That resource may be a beloved person or pet, a place (like your home), an object, or an activity. It helps you feel relief and well-being in your body; thinking about it can serve as a braking tool for a trigger or intrusive thought, without changing reality. Your sanctuary is another anchor that can provide protection for you.

What to Do

Take a moment to consider and answer these questions, perhaps in a journal.

- What is an object of sentimental value that is easily available to you? Perhaps something you could carry with you daily?

- What are some activities you could use as an anchor when intrusive thoughts arise, to help you focus on something other than the thought?

- What are your own personal anchors?

The key to using anchors successfully is that your anchors, whether they're objects or activities, are around and available to you when you're triggered. Next time you're triggered by something, try to take a few deep breaths. Use your anchor to focus your attention. This isn't about distraction, but rather maintaining a present focus on what's in front of you.

If your anchor is an object, try looking at it with fresh eyes. Turn it over, examine its textures and weight. See if you can notice something new about it you've never noticed before. Activity anchors are just as good. If you're using one, turn your attention to the movements your body is making. What feels good to do? What is a challenge? Can you do the activity in a slightly different way this time?

Distress About Distress

What to Know

It is common to feel distress about our distress. We feel guilty, sad, angry, or anxious about our sadness. But sadness plus anger, guilt, or anxiety does not equal less sadness; usually it adds up to more suffering for you and those around you. Guilt, sadness, anger, and anxiety: these feelings about feelings are what psychologists call *secondary emotional processes*. Many times throughout our lives, and especially during periods of grief, it is these secondary emotional processes that complicate and magnify our underlying distress. However, in the face of unconditional love and acceptance, even the most intense secondary emotional process can begin to melt away.

What to Do

If our secondary emotional processes are caused by distress reactions, those distress reactions are caused by particular triggers (especially in the first year after a loss). By becoming aware of what your triggers are—people, places, things, significant dates, or milestones that remind you of a lost loved one or a changed circumstance—you can allow yourself to become mindful and accepting of your distress. This does not mean rushing headlong into your suffering. It means allowing yourself to experience feelings as they arise, mindful of their causes, their impermanence, and your feelings about them. Knowing that you will meet these triggers and allowing yourself to go through them using radical acceptance is a core method of grieving mindfully.

For the next week, try to keep track of the people, places, things, significant dates, and milestones that trigger your sadness. Note how you felt using this structure: "I am feeling..."

It is important to name what you're feeling for what it is—an emotion. Bring a welcoming energy to your feeling; meet it with radical acceptance, allowing the feeling to be as it is, without judging it, so you can stop struggling with it and begin to heal. "I am okay feeling this way." "It makes sense that this feeling would come up because of this trigger, because..."

The more you are able to know, name, and track these feelings, the more the distress about your distress should dissipate. If it doesn't, try the next exercise.

Emotion Surfing

What to Know

Grief transforms us. It peels away masks, breaks the mind's habits, slows us down, takes us deep inside ourselves, rearranges our insides, churns up unresolved issues, and brings everything into question.

It can be humbling to realize that grief is so much more powerful than we are. We realize how fragile we are, how precious life is, how our lives can change in an instant. We will never return to the life we knew before the loss of a loved one. We will never be the same.

Feelings like grief can come in waves, arising out of our depths and bowling us over with their intensity. There are also periods of calm, even peace, in our lives after grief. Conflicting feelings can arise simultaneously. We never know what to expect. But how might grief, or any other emotion, work in us if we do not interfere with or resist these natural flows? In this activity, you'll learn *emotion surfing*—the skill of riding the waves of emotion as they come, letting them arise and pass, as all waves do.

What to Do

When you are feeling something particularly intense, take a few belly breaths, and take a moment to consider how your body is feeling. Is it tense? Sore? Anxious to move? Describe any sensation you're experiencing to yourself.

Then, focus on the emotions that accompany this sensation you're experiencing.

On a scale of 1 to 10, how intense are your emotions in this moment?

Do you have any intrusive thoughts (*I can't take this*, *This feeling is overwhelming*, *I feel so sad*) or urges to scream, cry, run away, or hide? What do these feelings make you want to do? Notice these too, like clouds billowing by or waves in your mind's ocean.

Imagine your feelings, and the thoughts and urges they compel, just being there. Imagine they're a wave, and you're the rider, moving with them as they pass. Inevitably, they will.

Now return to your breath. Feel your chest expand and contract with each breath. Count ten breaths. One on the inhale, two on the exhale.

On a scale of 1 to 10, how intense are your emotions in this moment?

Approach this as an experiment. Some days will be easier than others when it comes to surfing your emotions, rather than being over-whelmed by them. But if you can remember to stay mindful, even in the moments your grief is strongest, you'll find you can relate to that grief differently. It may become less acute than it does when you're fighting it or trying to make it go away.

Naming Your Fears

What to Know

It is not unusual to experience at least some resistance while you're processing your grief, even when you feel excited about the prospect of the healing that can come from it. It is normal to resist facing pain and intense feelings. We often avoid things that feel hard or scary. The key is to turn toward what you fear rather than against it. Acknowledge this resistance; don't ignore or fight it.

What to Do

Set a timer for two minutes. Name your fears; make a list of them. Here is an example.

I'm afraid of:

> *losing control*
>
> *crying so hard that I can't stop*
>
> *being overwhelmed*
>
> *falling into a bottomless pit*
>
> *becoming nonfunctional*
>
> *becoming paralyzed with the pain*
>
> *being left alone*

Once the two minutes are over, consider what the experience of naming your fears was like. Has it changed the shape of what you're feeling, or its intensity?

As healing progresses, you may need to use this exercise less frequently, but you should still use it from time to time to check in. This keeps you honest with your grief. Inevitably, you will find that, as you process your loss, the act of naming your fears will yield a very different experience from the one you feared you would have. You may discover that you don't feel overwhelmed by the feelings that surface. You may begin to experience your memories and experiences as a homecoming.

Whatever stage you're in on the journey to process grief, it's important to actively work to integrate and heal your grief, rather than just passively experience your reactions to it. This exercise offers you one way to do this.

Your Positive Traits

What to Know

As you think about all the experiences you have had, remember that you are still here and survived them and that you used many positive character traits to do so (Cohen, Barnes, and Rankin 1995). Leaning on these positive parts of yourself can be useful in tough times of grief or mourning, or even when you are simply feeling low.

What to Do

Think or journal about the following:

- How and when have you shown determination?

- How and when have you shown your will to persist and to eventually succeed?

- How and when has your faith helped you, particularly faith in yourself and your support system?

- How and when have you shown courage?

- How and when have you taken personal responsibility for meeting your needs?

- How and when have you exhibited your personal creativity?

- How and when have you shown your resilience?

- How and when have you used your intuition?

- How and when have you been able to maintain optimism?

- What other strengths can you identify within yourself that you've used in your life?

Thinking Your Way Through Grief

What to Know

When we experience a loss, it is common for the mind to try to find a way out of the pain. We go over and over what we could have said or done; we repeatedly review details of our last time together. This can lead to obsessive thinking, anxiety, and insomnia. We will not heal our grief if we stay at this mental level. We cannot think our way out of grief.

What's more, many of us carry certain beliefs about grieving:

- Grief will heal in time by itself.

- I should be back to normal after six weeks (or some other set period of time).

- If I am strong and stay busy, I will get through the grief without any repercussions.

- If I start crying, I will never stop.

- If I really heal and let go, I will lose my loved one forever.

However, our mind is highly influenced by the degree and intensity of our feelings—and our thoughts are really good at seeming like facts, when they are closer to wishes.

If you were to explore your own beliefs around grief, truly explore them, what would happen?

What to Do

What are your strongly held beliefs around grief? Write them down somewhere—say, in a journal.

These beliefs can lead to postponing or ignoring grief. And in so doing, they can seriously compromise our capacity for truly living. They can block the natural flow of healing that occurs after a loss.

As you turn toward your grief, what would it be like to grieve without your preconceptions and fears? Could you enter into relationship with this wise, healing force within you? What will you discover if you do?

Often, we discover that grief has its own nature, rhythm, and timing; it resists our attempts to control it. We also discover that grief involves more ongoing changes in our lives than we could have ever imagined. It can surprise us with its power, its unpredictable timing, its fathomless depth, its transformational potential, and the scope of change it brings into our lives.

If you find this exercise helpful, you might return to it, seeing how your grief might change as time passes.

Unravel Problematic Beliefs

What to Know

One of the most problematic things about experiencing grief is the way that our culture shapes our beliefs about how the experience *should* unfold. We are told to be instantly back at work, or to be able to stay present at our child's recital, or to suck it up and move on. These culturally informed beliefs and mandates then increase the degrees of our suffering by enhancing our levels of shame and guilt, ultimately impacting our lives in negative ways. The good news is that there are proven ways to unravel these beliefs about what we *should* do or how grief *should* be before they become a problem.

What to Do

What "shoulds" or self-punishing thoughts are you struggling with? Any negative beliefs you have may be challenged and modified if you choose to do so. This process is not always easy and may require a great deal of persistent effort. But it is possible.

If you want to challenge or dispute core beliefs, you have several options:

- You may look for evidence or proof that your belief is valid.

- You may find others and debate your belief with them.

- You may try to use imagery and visualization to change certain aspects of the belief.

You also may ask yourself the following questions to challenge your belief (partially adapted from Resick 1994):

- What is the evidence for and against the belief?

- Is the belief a habit or a fact?

- Is my interpretation of the situation accurate or not part of reality?

- Am I thinking in black-and-white or all-or-nothing ways?

- Are the words and phrases I am using extreme and exaggerated (such as "always," "forever," "must," "should," "ought," and "have to")?

- Am I making excuses?

- Is the source of information for my belief reliable?

- Am I thinking in terms of probabilities (shades of gray) or certainties (black and white)?

- Are my judgments based on feelings, not facts? Do I consider a feeling to be a fact?

- Is this belief my own, or does it come from or belong to someone else?

- Does it fit in with my priorities, values, and judgments?

- Does it make me feel bad?

- Is it hurtful to me?

- Is it hurtful to others?

- Is it appropriate in the demands it makes on me?

- Is it appropriate in the demands it makes on others?

- Is it considerate of me?

Feeling Your Feelings

What to Know

Learning how to use feelings to guide appropriate behavior is important. Grief can sometimes make us feel powerless in the face of our own emotions. Paradoxically, though, working hard to control how we feel has the potential to make us feel worse. It is important that you are able to experience both pleasant and unpleasant emotions without overreacting or underreacting, and that if things really get rough, you are able to self-soothe. The goal is for you to be able to look at possible ways to express your emotions and then make choices.

What to Do

What are some emotions you particularly struggle with? Try to think back to one or two specific situations from the past week or so where grief led you to respond in ways out of proportion to what was actually happening.

Consider (perhaps in your journal):

- What happened in each situation? What did you feel? And what did you do?

- Were there any feelings that felt "bad" to you—as though they were unacceptable, embarrassing, shameful, or too strong to be borne?

- Were any of these feelings ones that you may not enjoy having but are at least willing to accept having?

- Are there ways you can act differently when these feelings, even the tough ones, arise?

- Sometimes, we can exit a situation if we're feeling triggered, sensitive, or vulnerable, to give ourselves time to process and deal with overwhelm. Or perhaps you can let those around you know you're struggling and doing your best.

- How do you feel about your feelings right now? How would you *like* to feel about your feelings and your reactions to what life brings?

Expressing emotions honestly can bring about gratification, either immediately or over time, as you become more honest with yourself and others and as you let go of emotional baggage that has collected over time. Expressing an emotion means taking a chance—reaching out to others, communicating what you need, and perhaps risking another person's misunderstanding or incomprehension in the process. However, the end result—of being able to express yourself as honestly as you can to get your needs met as best you can—is worth that risk.

Your Support System

What to Know

When we lose something, it can initially be inconceivable that anyone understands the depth of our feeling. But this exact kind of thinking can lead us to isolate ourselves.

Research has shown the immense positive impact that social networks can play in helping us navigate and process our grief and loss (APA 2019). So whenever you are up for it, integrate your loss into your community of family and friends. Of course, relationships often change; unexpected people might show up to give you support, while others you had counted on might withdraw, probably out of their own discomfort with grief. You may find that you need more depth and authenticity in your relationships.

What to Do

Seek out others who can support you in your grief by providing safe witness and listening. The best kind of social support is just that: support. Use this rubric to keep an eye out for those who are allies in your grief journey.

They are people who can be with you

without judging,

without trying to fix you,

without giving you advice, and

without minimizing your experience.

When you give voice to your sorrow (with someone who can respectfully hold space for you), you share your humanity—and with it, the connectedness of all human suffering.

It's a relief to not try to be anyone else or anywhere else; it's a relief to allow ourselves to be exactly as we are, without judging ourselves. When we are able to meet ourselves in this way, we naturally feel at home in ourselves. We rest in being; we relax and begin to feel comfortable in our own skin. In the midst of our grieving, we feel present and whole—no longer divided.

PART 2

How to Process Loss

Much of the well-meaning wisdom on grief is that it takes time. But what do we do in the meantime? In reality, the journey of grief is winding and in some ways unending. Processing our grief in unhealthy ways has the potential to entrench us in problematic behaviors that take us away from the life we want and the person we wish to be. The tools in this section are about learning techniques to process your loss in a healthy manner that can help you move forward in soulful ways that build you up. It isn't always easy, but it is definitely worth it.

OUR LIVES ARE
BROKEN APART
AND
RECREATED IN
TIMES OF
GRIEF.

The Spiral Staircase

What to Know

As time goes on, most of your distressing feelings diminish in intensity. This can take months, or it can take years. You may find that some of your feelings linger just under the surface, waiting for an opportunity to present themselves. You may feel like you are waiting for someone or something, or you may feel vaguely upset or distressed. At times, you may also feel as though you can experience happiness and joy again. Over the course of time, you may find that your grieving process is marked more by the blues, or even periods of joy, than the intense emotions of acute grief. These feelings of general distress with islands of happiness, and the time between moments of acute grief, can be described as *subtle grief*.

When you experience subtle grief, you are able to go to work and carry on with your life, but you are still grieving. You may not even be aware that you are still experiencing grief; other people may notice in your stead, or you may realize it only a little later.

Acute and subtle grief alternate in a complex dance. This dance is the emotional roller coaster that is the grieving process, and it is what makes grief so unpredictable. When you have experienced subtle grief for a while, you may feel that you have come through the worst of it—and you may indeed be done with the worst of it. However, your hopes may be dashed when you experience intense acute grief again.

We often think of our emotional journeys as arcs—relatively linear passages from one state of being to the next. It may be more helpful to think of grief, in particular, as unfolding in a different shape: a spiral staircase.

What to Do

Because of how nonlinear the movement between acute and subtle grief can be, it is best described as a spiral instead of as a series of steps or a predictable line on a chart. Each circuit of the spiral represents a turning point in your relationship with the loved one you have lost and with your relationship to grief and is marked by a period or episode of acute grief. These circuits of the spiral also contain the emotional ups and downs of subtle grief, and when they occur, leaning on in-the-moment strategies like emotion surfing and radical acceptance (discussed in part 1 of the book) can provide structure and support for your feelings.

The important thing is that you commit to the process of loss. Through the committed practice of honoring your grief, each of these twists and turns gradually, sometimes imperceptibly, gets less exaggerated, leaving you feeling better than you did after the last one.

With each passing turn of acute grief in the spiral, no matter how many there may be, your relationship with grief and with the loved one or life you've lost changes. There may be periods of renewal; you will also inevitably experience feelings of intense sadness and loss that may seem like setbacks. You may even feel as if you are right back where you started. But most likely, you are actually making gradual progress up a staircase of growth.

Indeed, most people eventually come to see grief as a period of intense personal and spiritual growth. As you ascend the spiral staircase of grief, you may not always know where you're going—sometimes you feel better, sometimes worse—but you can know that the whole staircase is your evolutionary journey through grief.

Answering the Whys of Grief

What to Know

At one time or another, most people who have experienced a loss will find themselves asking *Why?*

Why have I experienced loss?

Why did this have to happen?

Why am I suffering?

Why does it hurt so much?

You may ask why your life has changed, why your relationship ended, why someone close to you has left, why you lost something that meant the world to you, why we die, or why we suffer. You may ask why the person you have lost did what they did, or why you didn't do something differently. You may be asking what point there is to life, what it all means, and why we are here.

These questions arise frequently in the midst of acute grief when there often seems to be no explanation to justify the existence of such pain.

What to Do

These questions are best answered personally instead of universally. That is, it is more important for you to find *your* answers to these questions, on *your* terms, than to try to figure out the meaning of life and loss for everyone. Even if you have come to terms with loss before, each relationship is unique. There may be new avenues for you to explore or new facets to discover. The meaning that you find in this particular experience of grief may emerge from something unexpected, forgotten, or new.

The answers to the riddle of your suffering—why you are experiencing it, what will get you through it, and how you will grow because of it—may also unfold over time. That is, over time you will probably find several answers to each of your "whys," instead of just one. So keep track of your answers. Make a habit of looking at these questions—say, at intervals of every three months—to explore how your answers to them are changing. Use your time in your sanctuary (see part 1) to reflect on them with a spirit of curiosity and openness. Sometimes, even these answers may seem inadequate. This is okay. It is best to allow yourself to accept different meanings as they arise, since each turn of the spiral staircase may bring with it new explanations for both the presence of suffering and how to endure it.

By now, it should be clear to you that there are no easy answers for why you are experiencing loss and what it all means within the scope of your life. In fact, human beings have been asking these same questions for thousands of years, through religion, science, and philosophy. These are humanity's attempts to explain life's basic mystery—why we, and all the things we experience, are subject to change, loss, and decay.

The Five Things

What to Know

Dr. Ira Byock, a pioneer in the American hospice movement, has talked extensively about "the five things" (1997): the topics that typically need to be covered in relationships and the messages we need to convey to one another in order to facilitate closure. These are *I'm sorry*, *I forgive you*, *Thank you*, *I love you*, and *Goodbye*. These five things cover all the emotional territory of any relationship. You might discuss them with your loved ones over days and months, even years, and whether the loved one is here or not. They can also be a part of any intentional grief practice. They are very useful in your sanctuary time, or anytime you're setting aside time in your day to process your emotions.

What to Do

As you read over these descriptions of the five things, try to recall instances when you were able to talk to your loved one about these themes, even when there was no intention of the communication being final.

The five things are:

1. *I'm sorry.* Everyone in a close relationship has some regrets. None of us is perfect, especially in the way we treat each other. Apologies are often spoken long before remorse is felt; out of a sense of duty, we may say "I'm sorry" long

before we feel it. But all apologies, whether big or small, hasty or well planned, pave the way for forgiveness. And if you were not able to truly apologize for something you regret, you may find some comfort in symbolically and intentionally asking for forgiveness now.

2. *I forgive you.* This can be forgiveness for anything and everything. Forgiveness can be thought of as radical acceptance toward someone else. Forgiveness is not to be confused with forgetting. However, when you forgive, through the power of compassion, you release the hold that this issue you're forgiving has had on your life. You take upon yourself the responsibility for living life on your terms, rather than feeling unresolved outrage or a sense of justice unserved.

3. *I love you.* Love is why you are grieving. Love transcends all sorrow, but sorrow can be fueled by love. Asking forgiveness and forgiving wrongs opens your heart to the full power of love. Acknowledging this love is an affirmation of the relationship, your grief, and your capacity to share yourself with another human being.

4. *Thank you.* What did you learn from this relationship? What was special about your time together? How did your life change as a result of your loved one's presence, or even loss? Perhaps you learned to love deeper than you had thought possible, or perhaps you learned how to change the oil in your car. This is what you can thank your loved one for.

5. *Goodbye.* There is hardly ever a right time to say goodbye. If you have already lost your loved one, saying goodbye after their loss is a recognition of their absence, your grief, and your having cherished their presence. Saying goodbye

to someone who is already gone does not dismiss that person from your life or mean that your grief is over. Remember, grief does not end, even though it may stop hurting. Grief only changes.

Particularly if you weren't able to actually address these topics with your loved one, whether because of the circumstances of the relationship or the type of loss, recalling or imagining yourself saying any of these five things to your loved one can help you to feel that the relationship was able to achieve a natural closure on some level. You can also try to have this conversation symbolically, such as in the form of a letter, visualization, or artwork.

The five things may be hard to say if you are idealizing your relationship. In many ways, saying the five things makes the loved one you've lost human again, instead of a focus of reverence or hatred. If any of these five things is difficult to express, it may indicate that issues related to that particular theme are standing in the way of your ability to find closure.

But even when it's hard, taking time to say the five things, out loud, in your mind, or on paper, allows you to develop a sense of closure in your shared relationship—a closure that comes from expressing your feelings, both good and bad, toward your loved one.

Even if you feel that your loved one cannot hear you, it is important to be able to articulate and express these five things for *yourself*. Ideally, the five things can be brought into your current relationships as well.

Pleasure, Pain, and Courage

What to Know

Often, distracted from our potential by our endless pursuits of pleasure and retreats from pain, we miss opportunities for growth. This wild-goose chase usually stops only when we are faced with the sense of helplessness that accompanies extreme distress. Most of the time, we feel entitled to pleasure, but experiencing pleasure also usually feels insufficient; you always still want more. It is only when we are distressed that we say, "Enough!" and turn to what really matters with clear eyes. Put another way, distress can motivate you to want to feel *better,* instead of *more.*

The world's spiritual traditions all seem to equate this sense of feeling better with feeling a connection to others. Distress inherently feels inharmonious; when you feel it, you usually want to reach out to others, or to feel soothed by a comforting friend, to restore your sense of belonging and connection.

In Buddhism, this sense of futility and helplessness is actually seen as the seed of equanimity—which is calm, peaceful acceptance of what *is,* rather than attraction to pleasure or aversion to distress; the ability to accept what we enjoy, but to do so being mindful of its impermanence; the ability to accept our emotional pain without being consumed by it.

In other words, achieving equanimity involves a practice of radical acceptance of what is, just as it is. The reality is that in order to not feel distress, you would need to stop feeling everything. This is the lesson of practicing equanimity: pleasure and pain actually have a lot in common. They are the two sides of the coin of our ability to feel. To deny ourselves the ability to feel grief or to avoid the emotions of grief would be to erode the essence of our wonderful human capacity for deep, intimate love.

Similarly, when you wallow in your misery, when your identity is your suffering and your suffering becomes your identity, you weaken the capacity to move away from pain and into healing. Although suffering may be painful, it becomes so familiar that you wouldn't know what to do with yourself if you did heal. You and your suffering become one, and you slowly forget your capacity to feel good or to make meaning from your pain.

By contrast, if you can cultivate a sense of equanimity even after the experience of loss, it can have a tremendous impact on how you live your life and relate to those around you.

What to Do

Both when we turn away from suffering and when we hold on to it tightly, the healthy expression of emotion is blocked. So, the way to move forward to equanimity is to:

1. Observe these tendencies, with the goal of simply allowing yourself to feel what you are feeling without imposing expectations or judgment.

2. Reorient your thinking to the possibility that these feelings are the fuel of your spiritual growth in grief. Can you courageously accept what you're feeling and use it as a spur to connect more deeply to your own experience and with others?

Dreaming of Your Loss

What to Know

If you're struggling with the loss of a loved one, know that you have significant power within yourself to create and recreate your relationships, to heal old wounds, and to experience deep intimacy. Your beloved is within reach—within you—much closer than you think. In the imagination, death does not end a relationship. And even as we practice accepting our loss in radical ways, it can be important to maintain a sense of connection with what you've lost.

It is in dreams that many have the first experience of their ongoing inner relationship with a deceased loved one. As you awaken from a dream about your loved one, you may think, *She's still alive!* and then realize your loved one has died. Our dreams seem to offer us the message that both are true: your loved one has died in the physical realm, but they are still alive within you.

Dreams arise from the unconscious and communicate important information about how grief is affecting us at this deep level of the psyche. They guide our work in the sanctuary as they confirm recent breakthroughs, alert us to what we are rejecting, and point out what we need to address in order to heal.

What to Know

If we approach dreams with respect, humility, and receptivity, we will build a constructive working relationship with the unconscious. We will remember more and more dreams; dreams will become more vivid and instructive.

In training yourself to remember your dreams, the first step is to place a pad of paper and pen by your bed. Go to sleep with the intention of remembering your dreams, along with the willingness to listen to their messages.

When you awaken in the morning, rest awhile in the threshold state between sleep and waking. Don't talk or get out of bed until you have recorded your dreams. If you awaken from a dream in the middle of the night, record it before going back to sleep. (As much as the conscious mind insists that you will remember the dream in the morning, you most likely won't.)

Start with brief notes that sketch out the dream (a few key words, not even sentences). Later that day, you can record the dream in more detail in your journal. Write out the dream in the present tense, as though it is happening right now. Don't edit as you write it down. An ordinary detail in the dream that you think is inconsequential may be much more significant than you realize. Give the dream a name.

Then, sit with the dream in your sanctuary. Hold the images softly in your awareness. Images that arise freshly from the unconscious in dreams have considerable power to heal and alter your consciousness—even without your understanding what they mean. Let the images work on you; feel their power. Let them come alive, without interpreting them. Approach the dream humbly, setting aside snap judgments. You may feel baffled or disturbed by the dream, which is natural when working with dreams.

Afterward, you might paint, draw, or sculpt the dream; dialogue with dream figures; act out the dream; or close your eyes and reenter the dream in order to explore one aspect more fully. Many people are shocked by how differently the deceased may appear in dreams—often they are younger, healthier, even happier, and more open than they were in life. It's as though the dream is reminding us that the relationship has changed.

Writing a Letter

What to Know

Are you struggling with feelings and sadness around a relationship that's ended—whatever the cause of the break? Writing a letter to a lost or deceased loved one gives you the freedom to express whatever you have held back or silenced in a relationship. Of course, your letter will likely never be sent to or read by the other person. The letter provides a safe place to unburden your heart—and the sanctuary could be a safe place to write it.

What to Do

You can start your letter in one session and continue it in subsequent sessions. Or you can complete a letter in one session. However you write it, express yourself fully, without editing your thoughts or feelings. Just allow what is stored inside to come out on the paper.

- What do you regret? Appreciate? Resent? Miss?

- What have you held back?

- What issues came between you?

- What are you ready to let go of? What do you want to carry on?

- What did you learn from this relationship?

- What promises did you make to this person?

- Is it time to reevaluate these promises?

At first, letters may be full of anger. That's okay. You may need to express uncomfortable feelings and thoughts before you can move on to feelings that are more loving or compassionate. Also, try to avoid blaming or preaching. The purpose is not to find fault with the other person or your situation; it is to express what is unresolved in your heart.

More to Do

If unresolved issues call for a deeper communication or understanding, you can explore writing a dialogue with your loved one. Start with a question and then—without letting your mind get in the way—write an answer. Stay with this rhythm of question-answer, question-answer until the flow of a dialogue begins to unfold.

As you reread your letter or dialogue, you might be surprised by the insights that emerge. It takes courage to suspend our normal mode of thinking and relax into the flow of communication and insight that comes from within. Be willing to let go and see what emerges and what rings true.

When you have finished writing for that day, read your letter. Feel where it has taken you in terms of healing.

- Did you express yourself freely, honestly, and fully?

- Did you address unresolved issues?

- Do you still have regrets?

- Did you express your love?

- Do you feel forgiveness, compassion, or tenderness?

Drop the Struggle

What to Know

If you've been trying hard for a long time to get rid of this emotional "stuff" and it's really taking a toll on you, it's time to try something different, a new way of responding to your feelings of grief and mourning. Dropping the struggle with difficult thoughts and feelings is the route to acceptance. Pushing them down through distraction, substance use, avoidance, or overthinking strategies is not a way to get rid of unwanted thoughts and feelings. Nor will dismissing or ignoring them make them "go away." Painful emotions hold valuable information, but we can't utilize that information if we're busy pushing them away, and our attempts to will away what's difficult only make those experiences more persistent.

What to Do

Imagine that at the back of our mind is a "struggle switch." When it's switched on, it means we're going to struggle against any physical or emotional pain that comes our way; whatever discomfort shows up, we'll try our best to get rid of it or avoid it.

Suppose what shows up is sadness. If your struggle switch is on, then you absolutely have to get rid of that feeling: *Here's that horrible feeling again. Why does it keep coming back? How do I get rid of it?* By this point, you've got anxiety about your sadness.

In other words, your emotional pain just got worse: *It's getting worse! Why does it do that?* Now you're even more anxious. Then you might get angry: *It's not fair. Why does this keep happening?* Or you might get depressed: *Not again. Why do I always feel like this?* And all these secondary emotions are useless, unpleasant, unhelpful, and a drain on your energy and vitality. And then—guess what? You get anxious or depressed about that! You can doubtless see the vicious cycle.

But now suppose your struggle switch is off. In that case, whatever feeling shows up, no matter how unpleasant, you don't struggle with it. When sadness, for instance, shows up, you might tell yourself, *Okay, here's a knot in my stomach. Here's tightness in my chest. Here's my mind telling me a bunch of scary stories.* And it's not that you like this or want it—it's still unpleasant—but you've resolved not to waste your time and energy struggling with it. Instead, you choose to take control of your arms and legs and put your energy into doing something that's meaningful and life enhancing—something that speaks to your values, even as you've acknowledged your sadness.

So with the struggle switch off, our sadness level is free to rise and fall as the situation dictates. Sometimes it'll be high, sometimes low; sometimes sadness will pass by very quickly, and sometimes it will hang around. But the great thing is, we're not wasting our time and energy struggling with it. So we can put our energy into doing other things that make our lives meaningful.

But switch it on, and it's like an emotional amplifier—we can have anger about our anger, anxiety about our anxiety, depression about our depression, or guilt about our guilt.

Without struggle, we get a natural level of discomfort—a level that's natural given who we are and what we're doing. But once we start struggling, our discomfort levels increase rapidly. Our emotions get bigger, and stickier, and messier; they hang around longer and have much more impact on our behavior. If we can learn how to turn off that struggle switch, it will make a big difference.

Breaking Bad Habits

What to Know

When in the throes of grief, mourning, or bereavement, it is common to find ourselves behaving in ways we aren't proud of. The emotional pain and turmoil of loss is intense, and it is perfectly human to adapt however we can to that. But to truly process your grief, you'll need to stop acting in ways that haven't felt like you. In order to do that, you'll need to take an honest look at your behavior.

Specifically, you'll need to know (a) what triggers your behavior and (b) what the immediate outcomes or consequences are. Triggers can include situations, thoughts, emotions, urges, sensations, memories; anything you can see, hear, touch, taste, and smell; and physiological states, such as thirst, hunger, illness, or fatigue.

If the immediate outcomes—the consequences—are such that the behavior continues or increases, they are known as *reinforcers*; they reinforce the behavior. Conversely, if the immediate outcomes are such that the behavior is reduced or discontinued, they are known as or *punishers*; they punish the behavior.

Once we know the triggers and consequences for any given behavior, we know the effects it has, or what it achieves, in a particular situation. For example, suppose that someone, alone in their apartment at night, has intense feelings of sadness that trigger them to drink. They have a drink, and the immediate outcomes are (a) their sadness disappears, and (b) they feel calmer or their pain is less acute. These outcomes keep the habit going so they are reinforcers.

We now know at least two reasons this person is drinking in this particular situation: to avoid sadness and to feel less pain.

What to Do

Are there problematic behaviors grief has led you to that you'd like to reduce or stop? You can use this four-step process.

1. **What triggers the behavior?** What situations, thoughts, and feelings typically trigger it? Are there particular people, places, events, activities, thoughts, memories, emotions, sensations, or physiological states that cue this behavior? Keep a diary: write down when and where you do the behavior you're hoping to stop and what you feel and think immediately beforehand.

2. **As you track this behavior, consider: What are the costs and benefits?** Any idea what's keeping this behavior going? Does it have any benefits you can identify? Perhaps it helps you get something you want, or it helps to save or protect you from something you don't want. Have you noticed any costs or drawbacks to this behavior? Any unintended negative consequences? Is there anything important that you lose or miss out on when you do this— important values or goals, or important people or activities in your life, that it distances you from? Does it lead to anything in your life that you don't really want?

3. **So if you don't do what you normally do when all that difficult stuff shows up, what will you do instead?** What's a good alternative? Write down a new behavior, once you're able to determine one, that's guided by what you value in life and the kind of person you want to be, not by what you fear—and consider:

- What values does this behavior serve? (See the "Living Your Values" exercise in part 3 of the book if you want more guidance on discovering and clarifying your values.)

- What difficult thoughts and feelings go with it? Are you willing to make room for them?

- Is this at least a seven out of ten, in terms of how realistic it is? If not, make it simpler and easier, until you can score at least seven.

4. **What skills are needed for you to practice your alternative behavior?** The ability to accept negative emotions? More time to practice mindfulness? Better flexibility? Be creative here. And know that determining what you really need is the first step toward getting yourself to those things.

PART 3

Finding Meaning Again

The moment we lose something is the moment our lives change forever. There is no getting around that. However, with our loss comes an amazing opportunity to reengage with living. This engagement is on our terms and driven by our values. Our losses can remind us of the preciousness of each day. It isn't about leaving someone behind and starting fresh, or forgetting or pushing past the loss you might feel for a time in your life that's passed, but using your memories of what or whom you've lost to reaffirm your commitment to the moment-by-moment of your life.

LOSS IS HARD.
IT CAN ALSO
MAKE ROOM
FOR
SOMETHING
NEW.

Living Your Values

What to Know

Values are desired qualities of behavior: the qualities you want to bring to your actions right now, and on an ongoing basis. Essentially, they're your heart's deepest desires for how you want to behave as a human being; how you want to treat yourself, others, and the world around you. In contrast to *goals*, which describe outcomes we are aiming for—what we want to have, get, or achieve in the future—*values* describe how we want to behave in this moment and on an ongoing basis.

This distinction matters because even when goals seem a long way off, or seemingly impossible due to our grief, it's empowering to live by our values, here and now. For example, a value such as "being kind" can underpin the smallest of actions (such as holding a door open for someone) to the largest long-term goals you have for your life. And while it may take you years to achieve long-term goals you might have, you can live the value of kindness every day, in a thousand ways, through things you say and do.

When we know our values, it helps us make better choices—do things that work better for us—even when we're racked by grief. They can serve as a sort of inner compass that can guide us through life, help us to find our way, and give us a sense of purpose. They also provide motivation and give us the strength and courage to do what really matters. When life is dull and gray, they add some color to it, and when you act on them, they give you a sense of fulfillment: a sense of being true to yourself, living life *your* way, behaving like the sort of person you really want to be, deep in your heart.

What to Do

What are your values? What are the qualities you want to bring to your day-to-day life—the ones that characterize the kind of person you want to be? Make a list of your values in your journal or in another private space. You might think of different domains of life—family, friendship, parenting, health, career, spirituality—and the qualities you want to embody in each: kindness, compassion, responsibility, courage, and so on.

From there, each morning, choose one or two values that you want to bring into play throughout the day. So, for example, you might pick "playfulness" and "openness." You can choose different ones each day or always keep them the same; it's up to you. Then, as you go through your day, look out for opportunities to "sprinkle" those values into your activities—so whatever you're saying or doing, see if you can give it the flavor of those values. And as you flavor it, savor it! Notice what you're doing and actively savor the experience—just like savoring your favorite food or music. Tune in, notice what's happening, and appreciate it.

What Matters Most

Grief clarifies what is important and what is not. It calls on you to recreate your life in a way that incorporates new perspectives, new priorities, and new values.

In a quiet moment, you might find that questions begin to surface from the upheaval inherent in grief—the deep questions that invite you to look at the quality and authenticity of your life. *What brings me joy? What is worth living for? What do I want?*

You may resist these questions at first; this is natural. It's not easy to reflect on our lives in this way. However, the process of questioning is one of the most creative aspects of the grieving process. It is these questions that will inspire you to look at what no longer sustains you, what is calling for your attention and energy, and where change is needed.

What to Do

When questions about your life start to show up, embrace them without trying to come up with the answers. Let the questioning itself move you deeper into yourself. Again, it is difficult to hold these questions in your consciousness without knowing where they are taking you; you naturally want to move away from that discomfort. You can use the nurturing environment of the sanctuary to connect with your own knowing, your inherent wisdom.

Some questions to explore:

- Am I living the life I really want?

- What do I need to let go of in my life that is no longer alive?

- What is sacred? ·

- Who or what do I love?

- What have I sacrificed in order to be successful?

- What is calling to me now in my life?

- How have I responded to or ignored that calling?

- What changes would I need to make in order for my life to truly sustain me?

- What new horizon in me wants to be seen?

If you let these questions work on you, your life will begin to open up in response—and gradually, answers may come. They could come in the silence of meditation, in a dream you had the night before, in a phrase you've just written in your journal or read in a book. Many times, these answers are accompanied by a sense of knowing—a tingling or shudder that you can feel in your body—an "aha" moment.

Sustaining New Habits

What to Know

To lose something big in our lives is to feel completely upended. Many people feel their routines and normal ways of life have shattered and find it hard to recover. Some find their ways into problematic habits. We're often eager—sometimes too eager—to reduce psychological suffering and build back a meaningful life. To achieve these outcomes requires patience and committed action: a commitment to living by and acting on our values, in ways both great and small.

Perhaps you're trying to set new habits for yourself, based on the examinations of triggers, behaviors, and consequences you've done in previous chapters, or your examination of your values, or just where you are in the grief process. If so, it's important to ask yourself, first:

- What values do you want to bring into play here?

- What do you want to stand for?

- What do you want to be about in the face of this grief you've been experiencing?

- What do you want to model for others?

What to Do

Start by identifying the new habit you want to set. Then break it down into the tried-and-true SMART goal template. Make sure your goal is:

S—Specific: Are you clear about exactly *what* you want to do?

M—Motivated by values: Is this action you wish to take a valued one?

A—Actionable: Is it something that can be done?

R—Realistic: Is this an action you can take given the resources and time you have?

T—Time-framed: Can you set yourself a time limit for making this change?

Make sure to also plan for obstacles you might encounter along the way as you implement this new habit and work to be consistent.

More to Do

Whenever you go through with your new habit, try—in the moment—to tune in to your underlying values and mindfully appreciate what happens as a result. This plays a big role in ongoing motivation. Sometimes, particularly in the early stages, you might feel as if you have to "white-knuckle" it, "tough it out," and "get through it" with little or no satisfaction or enjoyment. But even in these tough moments, work to notice and appreciate any time, no matter how brief, that you manage to be present, even in the difficulty. You'll find that even when the overall experience is stressful and dissatisfying, there are always moments within it you can appreciate. And over time, you are likely to have more of those meaningful moments, if you persist in practicing your new habit and in being mindful and patient with yourself as you do.

Explore Your Thoughts

What to Know

Most people think there is something wrong with them for "thinking negatively." In reality, though, your mind is a lot like everyone else's. The things your mind says to you are the same things others' minds say to them. Your mind is not damaged or broken. Your mind is not defective; there is nothing wrong with you for thinking the way you do. The thoughts you are having are normal, natural, and valid; we all have minds that think like this.

As it stands, you might find your mind is so preoccupied with thoughts of the past or the future; thoughts about your self-concepts and "who you are;" thoughts or memories of your grief; or reasons, rules, and judgments that it can make it hard to focus on the task at hand, engage in the activity you're doing, or be fully present with others.

One key to moving forward with your life is to see your thoughts for what they are: strings of words or pictures, changing from moment to moment, continually coming and going. It often feels as though the thoughts we have are true, and we often feel as though something must be done about them when they arise. But the reality is that they may or may not be true. And regardless of whether they are true or not, we don't have to obey them, follow their advice, treat them as threats, fight with them, avoid them, or give them our undivided attention.

What to Do

Instead of wrestling with your thoughts, which are fundamentally uncontrollable, or being held at their mercy, you can try a four-step process to truly explore and be with them: notice thoughts, name them, normalize them, and understand their purpose.

1. **Notice thoughts.** Simply notice the presence of thoughts. Ask, *What am I thinking right now?* Notice what your mind is doing right now. Is it silent or active? Or notice your thoughts: are they pictures or words or more like a voice in your head?

2. **Name them.** As you notice your thoughts, you can also name, or label, them. Initially, we tend to use generic terms like "thoughts," "thinking," and "mind." But, as you grow more used to this process and continue working through the grief you feel, you might try to get more specific or playful: *Here's the "unlovable" theme again, There goes "radio doom and gloom."* Or *I'm having the thought that...*

3. **Normalize them.** You could feel that there is something wrong with you for having so many "negative" or "weird" thoughts—especially if you've been told your thinking is "irrational," "distorted," or "dysfunctional." So, foster self-acceptance. You might say, *Thoughts like this are normal.* or *These thoughts make perfect sense given what I've gone through; they're a completely normal reaction.*

4. **Understand their purpose.** Ultimately, we can reframe even the most "negative," "problematic," or "unhelpful" thoughts by considering them in terms of the mind's purpose. Thoughts are the mind's attempts to protect us and meet our needs: to help us avoid what we don't want or get what we do want.

Below are a few examples of the kinds of distorting patterns our minds are prone to and what they may be intended to protect us against.

- **Worrying, catastrophizing, predicting the worst.** This is your mind trying to prepare you, to get you ready for action. It's saying, *Look out. Bad things are likely to happen. You might get hurt. You might suffer. Get ready. Prepare yourself. Protect yourself.*

- **Ruminating, dwelling on the past, self-blaming.** This is your mind trying to help you learn from past events. It's saying, *Bad stuff happened. And if you don't learn from this, it might happen again.* So you need to figure out: Why did it happen? What could you have done differently? You need to learn from this so you're ready and prepared and know what to do if something similar should ever happen again.

- **Self-criticism for recurrent problematic behavior.** This is your mind trying to help you change. It figures if it beats you up enough, you'll stop doing these things.

Try working with this four-step process for a few days or weeks. See if it makes any patterns of recurring negative thinking you're experiencing easier to deal with.

assiv

Taking a Stand

What to Know

There is no "right way" to grieve. There are no "right things" to do and no "right feelings" to have; there is no "right amount of time" to grieve for. Everyone finds their own unique way of grieving, and that will be hugely influenced by factors such as family history, cultural background, and religious or spiritual affiliations.

There are ideas out there that you *should* feel this, or you *shouldn't* feel that; or you *should* cry, or you *shouldn't* cry—and so on. And the truth is that there is no right or wrong way to feel when you're grieving. Some people feel angry. Others feel sad. Some feel guilty. Others feel numb. Some people even feel relief. And as with all emotions, they change like the weather: they rise and they fall; they come and they go. Everyone is free to grieve in their own way—to feel what they feel and to grieve for as long or as short as they wish.

What to Do

When you're experiencing grief, there's a massive *reality gap*: a huge chasm between the reality you want and the reality you've got right now. And most of us, at least initially, kind of get crushed by that reality gap, or we run and hide from it. But what we might do instead is turn toward this huge gaping hole—and choose to stand for something.

And it's totally up to you what you stand for—whether that's courage or honesty or compassion or love or anything else. Again, there's no right or wrong…it's just about being who you want to be, in the face of this pain.

Let's consider a few scenarios:

- Suppose an old friend bumps into you, six months from now, and asks you, "What did you stand for, back then, six months ago, in the face of that huge grief? How did you treat yourself and the people you love?" What would you want to answer?

- Suppose an old friend bumps into you, one year from now, and asks you, "What did you stand for, back then, a year ago, in the face of that huge grief? How did you treat yourself and the people you love?" What would you want to answer?

- Suppose an old friend bumps into you, five years from now, and asks you, "What did you stand for, back then, five years ago, in the face of that huge grief? How did you treat yourself and the people you love?" What would you want to answer?

Does answering these questions give you a sense of the trajectory you want to take—what you want to *do*, accepting that you're in the situation you're in?

Loss Is a Teacher

What to Know

Suffering can bring you to a place of profound mindfulness about your relationships and your spiritual beliefs. The people, relationships, and even times of life we've lost can be our spiritual teachers. It is not easy to deal with loss; we often wish we had not experienced it. But whatever it is you've lost had great meaning to you at one point in your life—likely has meaning for you still—and the process of grappling with the loss will have meaning for you too. Without the pain you're currently experiencing, you would not have the unique opportunity you now have to appreciate life and love and seek out personal growth.

Using the pain of loss as a spiritual teacher, you can begin to cultivate a sense of gratitude toward what you are feeling and experiencing. The intense emotional pain of your grief may still hurt. However, as you experience grief mindfully—allowing yourself to feel the twists and turns of the spiral staircase, the triggers and changes in your relationships, and your own personal development—you may eventually come to realize—mentally, emotionally, spiritually, perhaps even physically—that your capacity to grieve and your capacity to love are interconnected.

Grieving mindfully can therefore be an affirmation of life and of love. This is the challenge: to experience grief, hardship, and difficulty not as something shameful, impossible, punishing, or toxic, but as an opportunity to learn priceless life lessons.

What to Do

Take a few deep breaths and settle into your body. Bring your mind's attention to the thing that you lost: a person, a particular state or phase of your life, or something equally as profound. Focus on your relationship to what has been lost. Ask yourself how that thing you've lost, whatever it happens to be, existed—that is, what were its essential qualities? Were there parts of that person or situation that you especially loved? Were there parts that were challenging?

Now reflect on what role the person or thing you lost played in your life. What did they mean to you? What lessons are there about how you wish to live your life?

Finally, turn your attention to yourself. How are you experiencing this loss now? What do you feel? How are your days occupied? What can this loss teach you about this moment?

This spiritually minded attitude toward suffering changes how you think about life. You may find as you grieve mindfully, aware of what you are thinking and feeling, that you develop a deep confidence in your ability to live through pain. And your capacity to endure the inherent uncertainties of life only becomes more evolved and mature with time, and with diligent practice of mindfulness and mindful activities.

Reconstruct Your Future Self

What to Know

One of the things that gives us a sense of having a fixed, stable identity is the feeling that we know where we will be from one day to the next. In any relationship, there are expectations about future plans, which may be specific, such as plans to go to a certain place for a vacation, or abstract, like growing old together. In any case, these expectations about the future constitute what can be called a *future self*—an expected identity, one that you hope will be realized.

One of the reasons grief can feel disorienting is that when you lose something or someone, this future self becomes unraveled; all the plans you made are now impossible. As days pass—days that, for instance, you had hoped to share with a lost loved one—your loneliness may be all the more apparent.

Awareness of the unconscious tendency to project yourself into the future allows you to intentionally set healthy and positive goals for yourself, so that you can work to become the kind of person you want to be. Many people, in the process of losing a future self in this way, in fact come to realize that the future self and the present self are the same person—that is, who you will be tomorrow is a result of who you are today. Consequently, finding meaning in your pain involves asking yourself who you want to be as a result of your grief.

What to Do

Take a moment to imagine three specific things you want to do in the next year. Write them down somewhere that you can easily find them.

Next, set a reminder for three months from now. Another reminder for six months. And a final reminder for nine months.

At each reminder, use the opportunity to look at what you wrote. If you have already acted toward these goals you've set for yourself, use the reminder to find gratitude in that experience. Think about your favorite memory of the experience. If you haven't yet, do one thing in that moment to make that promise a reality for yourself.

Because it is one of the most emotionally intense experiences that human beings can have, grief can be disorienting. Your day-to-day life is drastically and unmistakably changed by loss. A veil of distress shrouds your past. Your future life is uncertain. However, grief provides a valuable opportunity to reorient yourself in the manner you see fit. There are many who, though overwhelmed at times by the pain of loss and separation from loved ones or old ways of life, are able to use the pain and distress of grief, like alchemists, to grow from their suffering. That is, they realize, months after they began feeling better, that their grief, though painful, has changed their lives for the better.

Learning from Nature

What to Know

The most burning questions about grief and about how grief changes your life have to do specifically with the emotional intensity of grief. What happens to the intense distress that accompanies grief, puts you at risk for depression, and has such life-changing potential?

In physics, the first law of thermodynamics states that energy can neither be created nor be destroyed. Energy can only be transformed. When massive stars many times more powerful than our sun are sucked into and crushed by cosmic black holes, their matter is released back into the universe in plumes of light and energy. The debris of these stars goes on to seed space, creating new stars, new planets, and perhaps even new life. From one of the most destructive forces in the universe come the building blocks and raw materials of life itself.

So too with grief. The energy of grief encompasses all that is your identity. Grief happens physically, emotionally, mentally, spiritually, and interpersonally. In another metaphor, the process of accepting loss and grief and letting it transform us becomes like a forest regenerating itself after a devastating forest fire—an event that is both catastrophic, in the impact it has on the forest in that moment, *and* just as much part of the natural order of ecosystems. Some trees even produce seeds that can only be opened by the intense heat of fire.

What to Do

Using nature as your guide, what metaphor from the natural world can you think of for your grief? Think of a natural process that involves loss and rebirth or transfiguration, or a cyclical natural process of depletion and restoration, like the changing of the seasons. Be as creative as you like.

My grief is…

An added bonus is to incorporate literal nature into your processing of grief. Make a routine of getting outside into spaces that are wild: city parks, hiking trails, gardens. There are numerous opportunities, no matter the context. Use the metaphor you created as a walking mantra as you move.

In this way, you make a commitment to yourself to engage the transformative power of grief with intention. You commit yourself to taking deliberate steps toward your future, ideal self.

The Challenge Formula

What to Know

In any challenging situation, no matter what it may be, we always have
two or three of the following options:

1. Leave.

2. Stay and live by our values: do whatever we can to improve
   the situation, make room for the inevitable pain, and treat
   ourselves kindly.

3. Stay and do things that either make no difference or make
   it worse.

Of course, option one—leave—isn't always available. For example,
if you've got a serious illness or lost a loved one, you can't simply leave
that situation; wherever you go, the problem goes with you. But, at
times, leaving *is* an option—in which case, seriously consider it. For
example, if you're in a toxic relationship, an awful job, or a profession
that exposes you repeatedly to traumatic events (e.g., emergency services or armed forces), consider: is your life likely to be richer, fuller,
and more meaningful if you leave than if you stay?

Now, if you can't leave or won't leave, you only have options two
and three. Unfortunately, for most of us, option three—stay and do
things that either make no difference or make the situation worse—
comes quite naturally. In challenging situations, we easily get hooked
by difficult thoughts and feelings and pulled into self-defeating patterns of behavior that, while understandable on an emotional level,

practically either keep us stuck or exacerbate our problems. For example, we may turn to excessively using drugs and alcohol, fighting with or withdrawing from loved ones, dropping out of important parts of life, or countless other self-defeating behaviors.

So the path to a better life lies in option two: stay and live by your values and do whatever you can to improve the situation. And of course, you can't expect to feel happy when you're in a really difficult situation; it's a given there will be painful thoughts and feelings. So the second part of option two—make room for the inevitable pain, and treat yourself kindly—is very relevant.

What to Do

The Challenge Formula is a fairly straightforward equation. It basically states that in times of difficulty, you will choose your future based on what matters most to you. So, use the formula below to create a strategic way of thinking next time things feel really hard:

- I feel _____.

- This feeling is painful and hard but also welcome, as part of a well-lived life.

- Instead of trying to make this go away, I want to welcome it.

- It reminds me that I should do one thing today in service to something that matters to me.

PART 4

Special Problems

There is nothing quite as destabilizing as losing someone or something you cared for deeply. For some, the force of the loss can tear apart much more than routines and our sense of safety in the world. Loss has the power to change how we eat, sleep, and interact with others. It can make us depressed, anxious, and even angry—it even has the power to alter our personalities. This is why it is important to acknowledge its impacts and seek remedies for problems associated with your grief.

WHEN YOU LEARN
TO ACCEPT HOW
GRIEF WORKS IN
YOU, YOU CAN
LEARN WHAT IT
WANTS TO SHOW
YOU.

Handling Feelings of Guilt and Self-Blame

Guilt is often part of the cluster of emotions that characterize depression. In grief after the loss of a loved one, in particular, guilt may also be fed by a sense of unfinished business in the relationship. When you feel guilty, you become absorbed in your own pain and your own low self-worth. And guilt does not easily allow for change. When feelings of guilt dominate your experience of grief, they become obstacles to your spiritual and personal growth. The relationship between pain and love becomes obscured and the potential for growth during grief becomes eclipsed by self-doubt, self-loathing, and self-blame.

Guilt makes it very difficult to seek solace and growth. To further complicate matters, guilt is almost always self-perpetuating. Most of us know that excessive guilt is not healthy, so we may even feel guilty about our guilt, and then we feel even worse about ourselves for "allowing" this cycle of guilt to take place.

Filled with self-blame, you may feel that life is miserable because it includes such suffering and that you have no potential for growth or development because you aren't worthy enough for such lofty goals.

What to Do

Take a few deep breaths and relax into your body. Bring up your feelings of guilt. The key in bringing them up is to hold them gently. Imagine they are a delicate glass globe that needs to be handled softly.

And then, seeing your guilt as it is, ask yourself: *What do I need to be forgiven for?*

Note: Forgiveness isn't forgetting. It's about radically accepting what you've been through and what you feel, allowing it to be there just as it is, and then, with compassion, choosing to release the hold that guilt has had on your life.

Now repeat slowly to yourself:

1. *I'm sorry.*

2. *I forgive myself unconditionally.*

3. *I love you.* Love is why you are grieving.

4. *Thank you for these feelings.* Remember that guilt is always an emotion associated with love.

5. *Goodbye.* It is time to leave these feelings of guilt aside. That doesn't mean you should avoid them. They will likely stay with you. But you are beginning to realize the purpose they serve and how committing to living your truth will ultimately make them less painful.

Is It Prolonged Grief Disorder or Is It Depression?

What to Know

The idea that grief can be experienced as personally and spiritually transformative is the central premise of this book. However, as creative and life-affirming as this task is, it is never easy, nor does it often feel very pleasant or enjoyable. This is very hard work, mainly because of the emotional intensity that comes with grief.

For many people, these disturbing thoughts and intense feelings are obstacles not only to transforming grief but also to living in general, and can often seem like depression.

What to Do

Here are a few important distinctions to examine and track within yourself:

Even though bereavement can feel like depression, a diagnosis of major depression is not usually given until at least two months after a loss. After two months, you may be diagnosed as having major depression instead of bereavement. Before the end of the two-month period, however, you may be diagnosed with major depression if you have certain symptoms:

- feelings of guilt that are unrelated to things you did or did not do at the time of death, such as medical decisions you had to make;

- certain types of thoughts about death;

- preoccupation with worthlessness;

- extreme fatigue to the point of not being able to do your normal activities;

- inability to do your normal, day-to-day activities for a long period of time, or not being able to do them nearly as well as you used to;

- hallucinating things other than your lost loved one.

A diagnosis of major depression requires that you have at least five of the following symptoms, including the first two:

1. depressed mood, reported by you or other people;

2. a significant decrease in interest or pleasure in almost all of your activities during most of the day, nearly every day;

3. significant weight loss or weight gain without any effort on your part, or increased or decreased appetite;

4. difficulty falling asleep or sleeping too much;

5. too much or too little activity, observed by other people;

6. fatigue or low energy nearly every day;

7. feeling worthless, or feeling excessive or inappropriate guilt nearly every day;

8. decreased concentration or ability to think, or being indecisive nearly every day; and

9. recurrent thoughts of death or suicide, attempts to commit suicide, or having a plan for suicide.

In addition to having at least five of the above symptoms, people diagnosed with major depression more than two months after their loss must also have these symptoms most of the day, nearly every day, for at least two weeks, and the symptoms must cause significant distress or impairment of normal functioning. If you meet these criteria, it is important to seek mental health treatment through your primary provider.

In our experience, when people are more depressed than grieving, they feel more hopeless about themselves and the future. They have a quality of apparent absolute helplessness—to the point that they become isolated or alienated from friends and family members—that is particular to depression more than grief.

Handling Anger and Rage

What to Know

When you've experienced loss, and there is no explanation that makes sense as to why the event happened, your anger may erupt, overshadowing your emotions of fear, grief, sadness, shame, or guilt. This anger may be directed at an individual. It may be directed at those who seem to have survived a similar event undamaged. Your anger may be directed at a system for its continued hurts, if you have to deal with law enforcement, the criminal justice system, attorneys, insurance companies, and even therapists. Your anger may erupt at the normal events of life that frustrate you rather than at the true sources of your anger. Your anger also may erupt toward yourself and your own body, particularly if you blame yourself for what happened. On the positive side, your anger also may motivate you to make changes in yourself or to work for a cause. Whatever it may be, it is important to assess. Giving anger time to defuse as you analyze it is a useful strategy.

What to Do

Think of a time when you were being hurt and had angry thoughts and emotions that you may have expressed inappropriately. Reimagine the situation using the prompts below.

1. I got angry because I believed…

2. I expressed anger by…

3. Perhaps I could not have done things differently because…

4. However, if there was something I could have done to express anger appropriately, I could have…

5. What patterns or triggers do I notice about my anger?

Anger can also be expressed appropriately and thereby accepted. In those instances that you choose to express anger appropriately, after examining the situation in question, you might ask yourself the following questions about your anger:

1. What message did that anger give to me?

2. What questions do I need to ask of my anger? What am I trying to protect or restore?

3. When has my anger become stuck?

4. When has my anger intensified into rageful explosions?

Experts say that anger may not lift until you learn to take specific actions to protect yourself. Sometimes, anger manifests as an expression of an entirely different emotion. Some of us may cry when we're angry, for instance, and others may express anger to mask sadness because it's uncomfortable to be vulnerable. Similarly, sometimes when anger is turned inward, it can be expressed as sadness or depression. Anger may also turn to shame and guilt when you become angry at yourself for violating others' boundaries.

When has your anger actually been frustration, which is a result of being ineffective? Frustration can also build to a point of rage.

Reflecting on the following questions may help you to deal with frustration:

- What is the message your frustration is sending?

- What can you do differently to resolve the frustration?

- Whom can you turn to for ideas or assistance?

Dealing with Worry

Does the grief or pain you feel drive you to worry—about things you feel are uncertain, situations that leave you stressed, your own capabilities, or what the future might bring? Pastor John Chadsey (2014) once noted that worry is unreasonable, unnatural, and unhealthy, in that it doesn't change the past or control the future, but it does mess you up today.

It can be hard to break yourself out of a cycle of worrying, especially when you're dealing with grief. But there are some ways you can work with your worries to make them less of a presence in your life.

What to Do

The next time you find yourself in the thick of worry thoughts (*What if…? What will I do when…? How can I cope?*), try to gauge if you have control over whatever it is you're worrying about. If you do have some control, to whatever degree, recognizing the agency you do have can help you break yourself out of your anxiety, or ease the pressure of your worries to some degree.

If you don't have control over what you're worried about, see if you can just let the worries go. We often fall into worry as a way of gaining control over whatever it is we're worried about—but often, that form of control is an illusion. Worrying about what might happen doesn't actually exert much influence on what does.

If you find it difficult to let go, try talking to someone you trust about those worries, to see if that perspective makes it easier to let go when you need to let go or to recognize control when you have it.

More to Do

Working to let go of your worries, rather than being at their mercy, will be good and helpful. You can also work to introduce more helpful and self-compassionate patterns of thought into your day-to-day life. One particularly helpful method for this, even if it's hard at first, is to practice gratitude.

What are some things in your life you're grateful for? Any number of things could qualify—people, places, good things that have happened to you today, good things you've done, your pets, your garden, memories you treasure—things, however large and small, that bring you joy.

Simple Communication Techniques

Relationships can be enhanced through effective communication. This involves talking directly with another person when something needs to be said. When you communicate effectively, you use clear messages that say what you mean; make statements when a statement is needed (rather than asking a question); clearly state your wants and feelings; do not intend to hurt the other person; and listen actively as well as talk.

What to Do

Asking questions. If you want to communicate with someone, you may want to ask probing questions to get better information about how the other person thinks or feels. *Probing questions* ask others to think and become more aware about what they have just said, and to clarify it. Asking a probing question does not mean that the other person was "wrong." In asking for clarification, you may ask the other person to explain something in particular, or you may say, "What do you mean by what you said?"

Describing feelings. Another basic communication skill is to describe your feelings by making an *I-statement*, such as "I feel happy when I am with you." The aim of making such a statement is to start a conversation that will improve your relationship. If someone is to take you and your feelings into account as worthy of consideration, they need to know how you feel. Describing feelings is a report on your inner state and gives information that can help build communication and a relationship.

Describing behavior. *Behavior description* is another basic skill for improving communication. If you use this skill, you report the specific, observable actions that the other person has done without valuing them as right or wrong, or bad or good:

> I've noticed over the last couple of days that every time I've offered a comment, all I've heard is disagreements and opposition.

The aim of behavior description is to open up discussion about how each person affects the other and about the relationship. When you use this skill, it is important that you describe the behavior clearly, using evidence and actions that are open to the observation of others. It's also important to avoid trying to infer beyond what you observe.

Active listening. When you listen actively, you listen with openness, as you try to see the other person's point of view. You listen with empathy, as you try to understand the other person's emotional state or feelings. And you listen with awareness, as you try to be aware of how what the person says fits with your known facts. As you listen, keep eye contact, maintain safe physical boundaries, and ask questions if you need to do so. Active listening also involves paraphrasing. When you *paraphrase* what another person says to you, you restate what you understand the other person's comment to mean. You do not just echo what the other person said but ask a question through which you test your understanding. For example, you may say some variation of the following: "If I hear you correctly, you're saying that you really don't want to go to the party tomorrow night because your ex-wife may be there. Am I right?"

Using humor. Using humor can help communication by relaxing tension, reducing bad feelings, increasing a feeling of fellowship, or reinforcing a point. Humor can also help you express feelings more openly and spontaneously. You may use exaggeration, irony, wordplay, or other types of humor. Humor should not be a way to attack the other person. It should be used with playfulness and should not evoke ridicule or sarcasm designed to hurt the other. When it's used well, humor can make a situation more joyful and can improve a relationship. Laughter is good for the immune system, it reduces stress hormones and, over a prolonged period of time, burns calories. It seems there are many reasons to laugh.

Using I-messages. An *I-message* is a specific, nonjudgmental message that focuses on the speaker, not the person listening. When you use an I-message, you describe how the other person's behavior is affecting you without blaming the other person. With an I-message, you state the behavior that affects you, how it affects you, and why, in three parts:

1. *When you* (state the behavior),

2. *I feel* (state the feeling),

3. *because* (state the consequences).

More to Do

Consider the following points of guidance for good listening.

1. Be quiet.

2. Give the other person your full attention. Meet their gaze; show them respect.

3. Show empathy with your words and your gestures.

4. Don't interrupt. Give the other person time to speak.

5. If strong feelings come up, don't act on them. Keep anger, confusion, or the desire to respond under control. Don't speak until it's your turn to speak. (And when you speak, do so as kindly and calmly as you can.)

6. When it's your turn to speak, use the communication techniques described above—probing questions, paraphrasing, describing emotions and behavior, and more.

The Relationship Contract

Many people who experience loss report that they no longer feel comfortable with other people, particularly if those other people haven't experienced the same kinds of loss. Also, you might have particular trouble relating to others if you've come to perceive certain situations to be unsafe, if you feel threatened, or if you have a history of being harmed by people you were encouraged to trust.

There are certain characteristics that make a relationship healthy. Some of them are as follows:

- mutual respect, empathy, and equality

- clear boundaries

- a balance of autonomy, dependence, and interdependence

- a continuous sense of the other person, even when they're not with you

- the use of negotiation to resolve difficulties

- basic trust

How do you feel about your relationships right now? With whom are you comfortable? With whom are you safe? To whom are you attached?

If there are people who you would like to keep in contact with, but you need new boundaries or need to set better expectations about your relationship with them, then you might be wise to write out a relationship contract. Or, if there are people who've particularly supported you in tough times, people you deeply value, this might be a good time to write them a thank-you note for all they've done.

What to Do

The following is a list of attributes people display in authentic relationships that you could draw from as you write out your relationship contracts or thank-you notes. People in authentic relationships:

- use emotion as information

- sit on uncomfortable emotions (their own and others'), without panicking

- sense and flow with the emotions of others, without panicking

- view misbehavior as a form of communication

- have boundaries that are sensitive, flexible, and responsive

- understand how shared emotions in a relationship work— which may include catching emotions from others, empathy, projection, transference, and conditioned emotional patterns

- resist the temptations to fix others in the relationship

- support others in the relationship and "hold the sacred space of possibility"

- see love as a commitment to treat the other with honor

- have a serving heart, focusing on serving others
- practice honest communication
- exhibit friendliness with others
- have patience
- see loyalty as a commitment
- unite with others in the relationship in shared purpose
- have fun and enjoyment

As for what these relationship contracts might look like, here's one example.

Dear [name],

I value our relationship. I also feel like some things in it may need to change. I'd like us to make some commitments about how we communicate and relate to each other.

I commit to

- Being clearer about my own needs and expectations

- Holding space for your emotions, especially when we're having tough conversations

- Letting you know when I'm not satisfied

- Working collaboratively with you on how things can improve when I'm not satisfied

- Treating you with honor and love

If you have expectations for our relationship, I'd like to hear them too.

Sincerely,

[Your name]

Having a Bedtime Plan

Often, when we're struggling with grief, we have trouble falling asleep or staying asleep. It's also possible for anyone to sleep better by improving their sleeping environment: by removing triggers from that environment, creating an atmosphere conducive to sleep, and using good sleep routines and practices. In other words, you can begin to change things that are possible to change.

What to Do

If you're struggling with your sleep, here's a list of ideas to try.

- Physically exercise sometime during the day (but not right before bed).

- Try not to drink anything in the two hours before going to bed, so you don't have to get up to go to the bathroom.

- Eat something light before bed, if you need to, and avoid caffeine.

- Take a walk in the late afternoon or early evening to tire yourself out and raise your body temperature. Falling body temperatures (after you stop your walk) sometimes make you sleepy.

- If you find you have trouble falling asleep because you worry a lot, schedule a "worry time" during the day and use up that time at least two hours before you plan to go to bed.

- Write or make an audio recording about your day (but not about any painful or traumatic experiences).

- Sleep in the same place; don't bed-hop or place-hop (the bed, not the living room couch, is for sleeping).

- Go to sleep and get up at a set time, and try to make it the same time every day, no matter what time you actually fall asleep. It'll help you set a good routine.

- Set the thermostat at a comfortable, cool temperature. Monitor that temperature.

- Listen to relaxing music.

- Listen to a relaxation audio recording.

- Practice relaxation techniques before going to bed.

- Pray.

- Medicate with prescribed medications or with the hormone/antioxidant melatonin, which can be used as a sleep aid.

- Talk to others if they can soothe you or calm you before you go to bed. Don't argue right before bed.

- Do a boring task.

- Read a very boring book.

- Use a night-light if necessary.

- Keep a record of the number of hours you sleep each day and how you feel after you have slept so that you can look for sleep patterns.

- Check with your doctor to see if any medications you are taking get in the way of sleep.

More to Do

It works best to create a routine that you stick to. The following is an example. But having self-compassion for your experiments—and understanding that if something is not working, it is not the end of the world—will do wonders.

1. Choose a regular bedtime that works for your needs, and then go to bed at this time for at least one week.

2. About two hours before that bedtime, do something relaxing. Use your sanctuary (see part 1), if you need it, to contain any experiences that might be triggering you.

3. Begin to get ready for bed at least an hour before your actual bedtime by doing your personal care routines (get your clothes out for the morning, brush your teeth, and so on).

4. Check out your room and make sure it is safe and comfortable: check your closets, windows, and doors; put away anything that might trigger nightmares, flashbacks, or intrusive thoughts (pictures, drawings, belongings).

5. Gather anything you want to have in bed with you (special cover, stuffed animal, pets).

6. Continue to contain any thoughts and feelings that might trouble you.

7. Use a relaxation technique to help you get to sleep.

8. Lie down and give yourself permission to sleep.

9. If you use music or another type of audio recording, turn it on.

10. Close your eyes and go for it.

Setting Emotional Boundaries

What to Know

Having emotional boundaries means that you are able to set limits without worrying whether or not you might hurt or disappoint another person. Asking for what you want or deserve is another way to set an emotional boundary. When you have good emotional boundaries, you can do this without worrying about whether you will be abandoned, disliked, hurt, or attacked. Grief can sometimes compromise our sense of our boundaries—both our ability to understand what we need and to communicate that to others.

What to Do

Part of setting boundaries is to create a personal "bill of rights." This bill of rights can allow you to set boundaries and take risks. Below are some personal rights people often choose to claim. Consider which ones you'd like to add to your bill of rights or create your own.

- I have the right to keep others out of my personal space.

- I have needs and can take steps to meet them or try to meet them.

- I have the right to express my feelings as I feel them.

- I have the right to make mistakes.

- I have the right to change my mind (and what I believe).

- I have the right to change who I am.

- I have the right to ask for help.

- I have the right to set a boundary.

- I have the right to be alone if I want to be.

- I have the right to let go of the past.

- I have the right to seek support from myself.

- I have the right to seek support from others.

- I have the right to set goals and then prioritize them.

- I have the right to give myself a compliment.

- I have the right to forgive myself when I am not perfect.

- I have the right to stop making unrealistic demands of myself.

- I have the right to stop blaming myself for things for which I was not responsible.

- I have the right to believe that I can succeed.

- I have the right to judge myself appropriately.

- I have the right to care for myself before giving to others.

- I have the right to say no to requests for intimacy or sex.

Once you have your bill of rights, you'll likely find it's easier to determine what you need and want, to say no firmly when it's right to say no, and to accept the reactions of those around you when you say no or ask for certain things to happen.

Diet and Exercise

What to Know

Simple lifestyle tweaks can be very effective for reducing stress. They often work even better when we improve our diet and exercise on a regular basis.

Your body needs minerals, vitamins, amino acids, good fats, and other building blocks to survive. Stress will deplete the body of these key factors and make your system work harder to manage stress. This also means that diet is one place you can intervene to help yourself feel better. Vegetables and fruits are full of fiber, minerals, and vitamins. Consider eating probiotic foods like sauerkraut and kimchi, and if you do not have issues with dairy, add yogurt and kefir. Also, note that not all fats are bad! Butter contains butyric acid, which is food for your gut lining. Avocados, coconut oil, and fish oil are building blocks for your brain and every membrane in your body (Bowthorpe 2014).

Maintaining a normal blood sugar is also important. When we are under stress, cortisol temporarily increases insulin resistance, which in turn makes more sugar in the blood immediately available to service the fight-or-flight response that kicks in when we encounter something we perceive as a threat. But chronic stress will lead to chronically elevated blood sugar, which can have consequences for how good we feel.

What to Do

You know your body, and your body will tell you what it needs. So, monitoring what kinds of foods leave you feeling tired, anxious, and annoyed will go a long way. Be mindful. Stick to the basics of nutrition with vegetables and fruits, whole grains, good protein, and balance. In addition, you could incorporate these suggestions:

- **Remove:** Take out foods that your body can't digest well.

- **Replace:** Add in digestive enzymes to help you break down your food completely.

- **Reinoculate:** Make sure you have good bacteria (probiotics) in your gut.

- **Repair:** It takes a minimum of two to three weeks for your gut to heal. L-glutamine and omega 3 fish oil are some of the supplements that can help.

More to Do

Exercise can help you regulate stress hormones and sleep cycles and manage your heart rate. At least thirty minutes of exercise daily, five days a week, is typically recommended; most of us don't have enough movement in our lives. Again, though, the important thing is to listen to your body. Sometimes, when we're stressed or grieving, more gentle forms of movement are better. You might try taking more walks, for instance, as a place to start. Or you can start with tai chi or yoga and then progress to harder workouts as you improve your fitness.

If you are completely exhausted after exercise and have to go to bed immediately afterward or find that you really can't function for the rest of the day, or if the exercise you're doing is leading to injury, then your exercise regimen is likely too much. Remember, your body needs to rest and repair. And working exercise into your life slowly and steadily is often a more sustainable course than doing too much too fast and burning out.

Conclusion

Throughout this book's journey, you've explored the rich emotional landscape of grief, its challenges and complications, and how it shapes the human experience. Whether it's the loss of a loved one, the end of a significant relationship, or even the grief caused by societal changes, processing this emotion is a fundamental aspect of our well-being. One of the core messages of this book is that feeling grief is far from being a burden; rather, there is profound strength and importance in properly processing our loss because it enables healing and personal growth, fosters resilience, strengthens communities, and brings forth compassion and understanding.

At the core of processing grief is the potential it has for healing your wounded heart. When we confront and embrace our grief, we embark on a journey of self-discovery, acknowledging our emotions and accepting the reality of loss. This process cannot be completed merely to escape from pain; it must be thought of as a courageous act of facing and integrating the complex emotions associated with loss. As many exercises herein have shown, using proven mental health tools allows us to experience a cathartic release of pain and emotions, which paves the way for healing.

The importance of processing grief becomes more evident as time goes on and we begin to find solace and meaning after loss. Through many of the self-reflection and introspection activities, you may have discovered new insights about yourselves and your relationships, finding a path toward acceptance and inner peace. This healing process is unique to each person, so go easy on yourself when comparing yours to others.

Another outcome of this process can often be personal growth. When we confront loss, we are confronted with the impermanence of life, prompting us to reevaluate our priorities and values. Loss often naturally begets a realignment of goals and aspirations. It compels us to face our vulnerabilities, and through this confrontation, build resilience and strength. By acknowledging our pain and working through it, we often find ourselves with more emotional maturity and a deeper understanding of ourselves and others. In turn, our journey with the mechanisms and emotional tools we used in this book can help us during future challenges.

There is also a profound understanding of the pain that others may be experiencing. Loss and pain help us to see others for who they are and what they've been through. This newfound empathy allows for deeper connections and the creation of more supportive networks that foster healing and growth for those around us. In a world that sometimes seems lonely and fractured, especially when we have lost something, the power of empathy and compassion that arises from processing grief can be a unifying force that brings all of us together.

This book has tried to give you the most essential tools for processing your loss. The hope is that it has been a good companion for you on your journey, and that at least one or two of the ideas in it stay with you. Whether you've just started it or you've been miles along, anytime is the right time to gather and use essential tools and skills for properly processing your grief.

Remember that healing is not about forgetting those we have lost either; rather, it is about integrating their memory into the fabric of our lives. They will forever remain a part of you (even as you will have other opportunities, and there is joy coming for you in the future) and the legacy of what is gone will continue to shape your story and inspire your actions.

Loss is inevitable and the feelings that come from the experience will come in spurts, waves, and by surprise. Remember that these experiences can be unique to you while at the same time shared by every one of us. You are not alone. Grief is a journey we must all embark upon at some point in our lives. It is likely not a journey you would have chosen, but it is one that you can navigate with courage, resilience, and compassion.

May you emerge from the depths of grief with a heart that is tender, resilient, and open to the beauty of life once more.

References

American Psychological Association [APA]. 2019. "Manage Stress: Strengthen Your Support Network." Last modified October 21, 2022. http://www.apa.org/topics/stress/manage-social-support.

Bowthorpe, J., ed. 2014. *Stop the Thyroid Madness II: How Thyroid Experts Are Challenging Ineffective Treatments and Improving the Lives of Patients*. Dolores, CO: Laughing Grape Publishing.

Byock, I. 1997. *Dying Well: Peace and Possibilities at the End of Life*. New York: Riverhead Books.

Chadsey, J., and J. Kim. 2014. "Happiness Can Be Learned Through Christ. The Habits of Happiness, Part 5." Sermon delivered at the United Methodist Church in Warrenton, Virginia, October 26.

Cohen, B. M., M. Barnes, and A. B. Rankin. 1995. *Managing Traumatic Stress Through Art: Drawing from the Center*. Baltimore, MD: Sidran Press.

Lichtenthal, W. G., and D. G. Cruess. 2010. "Effects of Directed Written Disclosure on Grief and Distress Symptoms Among Bereaved Individuals." *Death Studies* 34(6): 475–499.

Resick, P. A. 1994. "Cognitive Processing Therapy (CPT) for Rape-Related PTSD and Depression." *NC-PTSD Clinical Quarterly* 4(3/4): 1, 3–5.

Rothschild, B. 2000. *The Body Remembers: The Psychophysiology of Trauma and Trauma Treatment*. New York: W. W. Norton.

Van der Oord, S., S. Lucassen, A. A. Van Emmerik, and P. M. Emmelkamp. 2010. "Treatment of Post-Traumatic Stress Disorder in Children Using Cognitive Behavioural Writing Therapy." *Clinical Psychology and Psychotherapy* 17(3): 240–249.

Russ Harris is an internationally acclaimed acceptance and commitment therapy (ACT) trainer, and author of the best-selling ACT-based self-help book, *The Happiness Trap*, which has sold more than one million copies and been published in thirty languages. He is widely renowned for his ability to teach ACT in a way that is simple, clear, and fun—yet extremely practical.

Alexandra Kennedy, MA, LMFT, is a psychotherapist in private practice for forty-eight years; and author of *Losing a Parent*, *The Infinite Thread*, and *How Did I Miss All This Before?*. She has taught at John F. Kennedy University; the University of California, Santa Cruz Extension; and the Institute of Transpersonal Psychology. She has been interviewed in *USA Today*, *The Mercury News*, *San Francisco Examiner*, and *Boston Herald*, as well as on NPR's *Talk of the Nation*, CNN's *Sonja Live*, and KQED's *Family Talk* and *New Dimensions Radio*.

Sameet M. Kumar, PhD, is a psychologist at the Memorial Healthcare System Cancer Institute in Broward County, FL; with over a decade of experience working with end-of-life and bereavement. He is author of *Grieving Mindfully*, as well as *The Mindful Path Through Worry and Rumination*.

Mary Beth Williams, PhD, LCSW, CTS, is an author, researcher, lecturer, and trainer in the area of trauma. In addition, she treats trauma survivors in private practice at the Trauma Recovery Education and Counseling Center in Warrenton, VA. Williams is former president of the Association of Traumatic Stress Specialists. She is a trainer for US Customs and Border Protection; cofounder of the proposed 501(c)(3) US Vet Source; and author of many articles, chapters, and books about trauma disorders.

Soili Poijula, PhD, is a clinical psychologist, licensed psychotherapist, and director at Oy Synolon Ltd., a center for trauma psychology in Finland, where she has done pioneering work as a developer of post-trauma psychotherapy.

Real change *is* possible

For more than forty-five years, New Harbinger has published proven-effective self-help books and pioneering workbooks to help readers of all ages and backgrounds improve mental health and well-being, and achieve lasting personal growth. In addition, our spirituality books offer profound guidance for deepening awareness and cultivating healing, self-discovery, and fulfillment.

Founded by psychologist Matthew McKay and Patrick Fanning, New Harbinger is proud to be an independent, employee-owned company. Our books reflect our core values of integrity, innovation, commitment, sustainability, compassion, and trust. Written by leaders in the field and recommended by therapists worldwide, New Harbinger books are practical, accessible, and provide real tools for real change.

newharbingerpublications

MORE BOOKS from
NEW HARBINGER PUBLICATIONS

**PUT YOUR
ANXIETY HERE**

A Creative Guided Journal to
Relieve Stress and Find Calm

978-1648481451 / US $18.95

**HEAL YOUR PAST TO
MANIFEST YOUR FUTURE**

Trauma-Informed Practices to
Release Emotional Blocks and
Open to Life's Possibilities

978-1648483042 / US $21.95

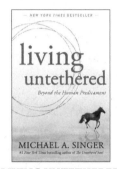

LIVING UNTETHERED

Beyond the Human
Predicament

978-1648480935 / US $18.95

**THE EMOTIONALLY
EXHAUSTED WOMAN**

Why You're Feeling
Depleted and How to Get
What You Need

978-1648480157 / US $18.95

**WIRED FOR LOVE,
SECOND EDITION**

How Understanding Your Partner's
Brain and Attachment Style Can Help
You Defuse Conflict and
Build a Secure Relationship

978-1648482960 / US $19.95

**SIMPLE WAYS TO
UNWIND WITHOUT
ALCOHOL**

50 Tips to Drink Less
and Enjoy More

978-1648482342 / US $18.95

🌱 **newharbinger**publications

1-800-748-6273 / newharbinger.com

(VISA, MC, AMEX / prices subject to change without notice)

Follow Us 📷 📘 🐦 📺 📌 💼

Don't miss out on new books from New Harbinger.
Subscribe to our email list at **newharbinger.com/subscribe** ✍